Rat-a-Tat

Alphabet Soup

A Phonics Reader

By Sasha Quinton

The Book Shop, Ltd.
New York, New York

A **fat** old dog **napped flat** on a **mat**.
Pitter-pitter**-pat**, up walked a **cat.**

Pitter-pitter-pat

She **sat** on the **mat** in a pretty party **hat.**
She woke the **fat** dog with a soft little **pat.**

Rap, tap, tap. "Wake up," said the **cat.**
"You **can't** go out to a party like **that.**"

"**Scat!**" said the **fat** old dog to the **cat.**
"Leave me alone to **nap** on my **mat!**"

Then **rat**-a-**tat-tat,** up walked a **rat.**
He **sat** on the **mat and admired cat's hat.**

"Dog!" said the **rat,** "Look **at that hat!**"
"You need a **cap that** is **snappy** like **that!**"

"**Scram!**" **snapped** the **fat** old dog to the **rat.**
"I don't **want** to **chat.** Get off of my **mat!**"

As the dog **napped,** the **rat and** the **cat**
Looked through a **basket** to find him a **hat.**

They put on a **tam.** They tried **a straw hat.**

They found one **hat that** looked like a **cat!**

Some **hats had straps.**
Some **hats had flaps.**

Some **had** spots, **sparkles, and snaps.**

And just when the dog woke up from his **nap,**
The **cat and** the **rat** found just the right **cap.**

"**Tada!**" said the **cat,** "How about **that?**"
"How about a **flashy** and **splashy** top **hat!**"

"Not **bad!**" said the dog. "I will wear this **hat.**"
Then **rat-a-tat-tat,** he jumped off of his **mat.**